GW00337666

THE ILLUSTRATED POETS

Shakespeare

EDITED BY
Daniel Burnstone

||| ·PARRAGON· |||

This edition first published by Parragon Books Ltd in 1995

Produced by
Magpie Books Ltd, 7 Kensington Church Court
London W8 4SP

Cover picture: The 'Flower' Portrait from the RSC
Collection with permission of the Governors of the Royal
Shakespeare Theatre. Illustrations courtesy of: Mary Evans
Picture Library; Christies Images.

ISBN 0 75250 031 7

A copy of the British Library Cataloguing in Publication
Data is available from the British Library.

Typeset by Hewer Text Composition Services, Edinburgh
Printed in Singapore by Printlink International Co.

Contents

Villains	1
Murder	15
Fortune	30
Life	38
Age	50
Time	64

❧ VILLAINS ❧

Glo.

Now is the winter of our discontent
Made glorious summer by this sun
of York;
And all the clouds that lour'd upon our
house
In the deep bosom of the ocean buried.
Now are our brows bound with victorious
wreaths;
Our bruised arms hung up for monuments;
Our stern alarums chang'd to merry
meetings,
Our dreadful marches to delightful measures.
Grim-visag'd war hath smooth'd his
wrinkled front,
And now, instead of mounting barbed steeds
To fright the souls of fearful adversaries,
He capers nimbly in a lady's chamber

To the lascivious pleasing of a lute.
But I – that am not shap'd for sportive tricks,
Nor made to court an amorous looking-
>glass –
I – that am rudely stamp'd, and want love's
>majesty
To strut before a wanton ambling nymph –
I – that am curtail'd of this fair proportion,
Cheated of feature by dissembling nature,
Deform'd, unfinish'd, sent before my time
Into this breathing world scarce half made
>up,
And that so lamely and unfashionable
That dogs bark at me as I halt by them –
Why, I, in this weak piping time of peace,
Have no delight to pass away the time,
Unless to spy my shadow in the sun

And descant on mine own deformity.
And therefore, since I cannot prove a lover
To entertain these fair well-spoken days,
I am determined to prove a villain
And hate the idle pleasures of these days.
Plots have I laid, inductions dangerous,
By drunken prophecies, libels, and dreams,
To set my brother Clarence and the King
In deadly hate the one against the other;
And if King Edward be as true and just
As I am subtle, false, and treacherous,
This day should Clarence closely be mew'd
        up —
About a prophecy which says that G
Of Edward's heirs the murderer shall be.
Dive, thoughts, down to my soul. Here
        Clarence comes.

Richard III

3

O villain, villain, smiling, damned villain!
My tables – meet it is I set it down
That one may smile, and smile, and be a villain;
At least I am sure it may be so in Denmark.

Hamlet

Edm.

This is the excellent foppery of the world, that, when we are sick in fortune, often the surfeits of our own behaviour, we make guilty of our disasters the sun, the moon, and stars; as if we were villains on necessity; fools by heavenly compulsion; knaves, thieves, and treachers, by spherical predominance; drunkards, liars, and adulterers, by an enforc'd obedience of planetary influence; and all that we are evil in, by a divine thrusting on – an admirable evasion of whoremaster man, to lay his goatish disposition on the charge of a star!

My father compounded with my mother under the Dragon's tail, and my nativity was under Ursa Major, so that it follows I am rough and lecherous. Fut, I should have been that I am, had the maidenliest star in the firmament twinkled on my bastardizing. Edgar!

King Lear

Glo.

I do the wrong, and first begin to brawl.
  The secret mischiefs that I set abroach
I lay unto the grievous charge of others.
Clarence, who I indeed have cast in
            darkness,
I do beweep to many simple gulls;
Namely, to Derby, Hastings, Buckingham;
And tell them 'tis the Queen and her allies
That stir the King against the Duke my
            brother.
Now they believe it, and withal whet me
To be reveng'd on Rivers, Dorset, Grey;

But then I sigh and, with a piece of
        Scripture,
Tell them that God bids us do good for evil.
And thus I clothe my naked villainy
With odd old ends stol'n forth of holy writ,
And seem a saint when most I play the devil.
                    Richard III

Iago.

V irtue? A fig! 'Tis in ourselves that we
    are thus or thus. Our bodies are our
gardens to the which our wills are gardeners;
so that if we will plant nettles or sow lettuce,
set hyssop and weed up thyme, supply it with
one gender of herbs or distract it with many,
either to have it sterile with idleness or
manur'd with industry – why, the power
and corrigible authority of this lies in our
wills.

Othello

Ant. [*Aside*]

M ark you this, Bassanio,
The devil can cite Scripture for his
purpose.
An evil soul producing holy witness
Is like a villain with a smiling cheek,
A goodly apple rotten at the heart.
O, what a goodly outside falsehood hath!

Merchant of Venice

Iago.

And what's he then that says I play the
villain,
When this advice I give is free and honest,
Probal to thinking, and indeed the course
To win the Moor again? For 'tis most easy
Th'inclining Desdemona to subdue
In any honest suit. She's framed as fruitful
As the free elements. And then for her
To win the Moor, were't to renounce his
baptism,
All seals and symbols of redeeméd sin,
His soul is so enfettered to her love
That she may make, unmake, do what she
list,
Even as her appetite shall play the god
With his weak function. How am I then a
villain

To counsel Cassio to this parallel course,
Directly to his good? Divinity of hell!
When devils will the blackest sins put on,
They do suggest at first with heavenly shows,
As I do now; for while this honest fool
Plies Desdemona to repair his fortunes,
And she for him pleads strongly to the Moor,
I'll pour this pestilence into his ear,
That she repeals him for her body's lust;
And by how much she strives to do him
        good,
She shall undo her credit with the Moor.
So will I turn her virtue into pitch,
And out of her own goodness make the net
That shall enmesh them all.

                               Othello

O coward conscience, how dost thou
   afflict me!
The lights burn blue. It is now dead
         midnight.
Cold fearful drops stand on my trembling
         flesh.
What do I fear? Myself? There's none else by.
Richard loves Richard; that is, I am I.
Is there a murderer here? No – yes, I am.
Then fly. What, from myself? Great reason
         why –
Lest I revenge. What, myself upon myself!
Alack, I love myself. Wherefore? For any
         good
That I myself have done unto myself?
O, no! Alas, I rather hate myself
For hateful deeds committed by myself!
I am a villain; yet I lie, I am not.
Fool, of thyself speak well. Fool, do not
         flatter.

William Shakespeare

My conscience hath a thousand several
        tongues,
And every tongue brings in a several tale,
And every tale condemns me for a villain.
Perjury, perjury, in the high'st degree;
Murder, stern murder, in the dir'st degree;
All several sins, all us'd in each degree,
Throng to the bar, crying all 'Guilty! guilty!'
I shall despair. There is no creature loves me;
And if I die no soul will pity me:
And wherefore should they, since that I
        myself
Find in myself no pity to myself?
Methought the souls of all that I had
        murder'd
Came to my tent, and every one did threat
To-morrow's vengeance on the head of
        Richard.

                       Richard III

❧ MURDER ❧

[*Aside*]

This supernatural soliciting
Cannot be ill; cannnot be good. If ill,
Why hath it given me earnest of success,
Commencing in a truth? I am Thane of
        Cawdor.
If good, why do I yield to that suggestion
Whose horrid image doth unfix my hair
And make my seated heart knock at my ribs
Against the use of nature? Present fears
Are less than horrible imaginings.
My thought, whose murder yet is but
        fantastical,
Shakes so my single state of man
That function is smother'd in surmise,
And nothing is but what is not.

                                Macbeth

W hy, I can smile, and murder whiles I
smile,
And cry 'Content!' to that which grieves my
heart,
And wet my cheeks with artificial tears,
And frame my face to all occasions.
I'll drown more sailors than the mermaid
shall;
I'll slay more gazers than the basilisk;
I'll play the orator as well as Nestor,
Deceive more slily than Ulysses could,
And, like a Sinon, take another Troy.
I can add colours to the chameleon,
Change shapes with Protheus for advantages,
And set the murderous Machiavel to school.
Can I do this, and cannot get a crown?
Tut, were it farther off, I'll pluck it down.

[*Exit.*
Henry VI Part 3

Then enter MACBETH.

Macb.

If it were done when 'tis done, then
'twere well
It were done quickly. If th' assassination
Could trammel up the consequence, and
catch,
With his surcease, success; that but this blow
Might be the be-all and the end-all here –
But here upon this bank and shoal of time –
We'd jump the life to come. But in these
cases
We still have judgment here, that we but
teach
Bloody instructions, which being taught
return
To plague th' inventor. This even-handed
justice
Commends th' ingredience of our poison'd
chalice

Othello with Desdemona and her father

To our own lips. He's here in double trust:
First, as I am his kinsman and his subject –
Strong both against the deed; then, as his host,
Who should against his murderer shut the door,
Not bear the knife myself. Besides, this Duncan
Hath borne his faculties so meek, hath been
So clear in his great office, that his virtues
Will plead like angels, trumpet-tongu'd,
        against
The deep damnation of his taking-off;
And pity, like a naked new-born babe,
Striding the blast, or heaven's cherubin hors'd
Upon the sightless couriers of the air,
Shall blow the horrid deed in every eye,
That tears shall drown the wind. I have no
        spur
To prick the sides of my intent, but only
Vaulting ambition, which o'er-leaps itself,
And falls on th' other.

Macbeth

[*Exit Servant.*

Is this a dagger which I see before me,
The handle toward my hand? Come, let me
      clutch thee.
I have thee not, and yet I see thee still.
Art thou not, fatal vision, sensible
To feeling as to sight? or art thou but
A dagger of the mind, a false creation,
Proceeding from the heat-oppressed brain?
I see thee yet, in form as palpable
As this which now I draw.
Thou marshall'st me the way that I was
      going;
And such an instrument I was to use.

Laurence Olivier as Hamlet

Mine eyes are made the fools o' th' other
      senses,
Or else worth all the rest. I see thee still;
And on thy blade and dudgeon gouts of
      blood,
Which was not so before. There's no such
      thing:
It is the bloody business which informs
Thus to mine eyes. Now o'er the one half-
      world
Nature seems dead, and wicked dreams
      abuse
The curtain'd sleep; now witchcraft
      celebrates
Pale Hecate's offerings; and wither'd
      murder,
Alarum'd by his sentinel, the wolf,

Whose howl's his watch, thus with his
        stealthy pace,
With Tarquin's ravishing strides, towards his
        design
Moves like a ghost. Thou sure and firmset
        earth,
Hear not my steps which way they walk, for
        fear
Thy very stones prate of my whereabout
And take the present horror from the time,
Which now suits with it. Whiles I threat, he
        lives;
Words to the heat of deeds too cold breath
        gives.   [*A bell rings.*
I go, and it is done; the bell invites me.
Hear it not, Duncan, for it is a knell
That summons thee to heaven or to hell.
[*Exit.*

Macbeth

Macb.

Methought I heard a voice cry 'Sleep
no more;
Macbeth does murder sleep' – the innocent
sleep,
Sleep that knits up the ravell'd sleave of care,
The death of each day's life, sore labour's
bath,
Balm of hurt minds, great nature's second
course,
Chief nourisher in life's feast.

Macbeth

Corn. Where hast thou sent the King?

Glo.   To Dover.

Reg. Wherefore to Dover? Wast thou not
          charg'd at peril –

Corn. Wherefore to Dover? Let him first
          answer that.

Glo. I am tied to the stake, and I must stand
          the course.

Reg. Wherefore to Dover?

Glo. Because I would not see thy cruel nails
Pluck out his poor old eyes; nor thy fierce
          sister
In his anointed flesh rash boarish fangs.
The sea, with such a storm as his bare head
In hell-black night endur'd, would have
          buoy'd up
And quench'd the stelled fires.
Yet, poor old heart, he holp the heavens to
          rain.

Lady Macbeth wills her husband to murder
Duncan

If wolves had at thy gate howl'd that dern
      time.
Thou shouldst have said 'Good porter, turn
      the key'.
All cruels else subscribe, but I shall see
The winged vengeance overtake such
      children.
Corn. See't shalt thou never. Fellows, hold
      the chair.
Upon these eyes of thine I'll set my foot.
Glo. He that will think to live till he be old,
Give me some help! – O cruel! O you gods!
Reg. One side will mock another; th' other
      too.
Corn. If you see vengeance –
1 *Serv.*   Hold your hand, my lord.
I have serv'd you ever since I was a child;
But better service have I never done you,
Than now to bid you hold.
Reg.   How now, you dog!

1 *Serv.* If you did wear a beard upon your
　　　　chin
I'd shake it on this quarrel. What do you
　　　　mean?
Corn. My villain!　　　　[*They draw and fight.*
1 *Serv.* Nay, then come on, and take the
　　　　chance of anger.
　　　　　　　　[*Cornwall is wounded*
Reg. Give me thy sword. A peasant stand up
　　　　thus! [*She takes a sword and stabs him
　　　　from behind.*
1 *Serv.* O, I am slain! My lord, you have one
　　　　eye left
To see some mischief on him. O!　　　[*Dies.*
Corn. Lest it see more, prevent it. Out vile
　　　　jelly!
Where is thy lustre now?

　　　　　　　　　　　　King Lear

The murder of Julius Caesar

Sleeping within my orchard,
My custom always of the afternoon,
Upon my secure hour thy uncle stole,
With juice of cursed hebona in a vial,
And in the porches of my ears did pour
The leperous distilment; whose effect
Holds such an enmity with blood of man
That swift as quicksilver it courses through
The natural gates and alleys of the body;
And with a sudden vigour it doth posset
And curd, like eager droppings into milk,
The thin and wholesome blood. So did it
    mine;
And a most instant tetter bark'd about,
Most lazar-like, with vile and loathsome
    crust,
All my smooth body.
Thus was I, sleeping, by a brother's hand
Of life, of crown, of queen, at once
    dispatch'd;

Cut off even in the blossoms of my sin,
Unhous'led, disappointed, unanel'd;
No reck'ning made, but sent to my account
With all my imperfections on my head.
O, horrible! O, horrible! most horrible!
If thou hast nature in thee, bear it not;
Let not the royal bed of Denmark be
A couch for luxury and damned incest.
But, howsomever thou pursuest this act,
Taint not thy mind, nor let thy soul contrive
Against thy mother aught; leave her to
        heaven,
And to those thorns that in her bosom lodge
To prick and sting her. Fare thee well at
        once.
The glowworm shows the matin to be near,
And gins to pale his uneffectual fire.
Adieu, adieu, adieu! Remember me.   [*Exit.*
        Hamlet

Keep. What was your dream, my lord? I pray
    you tell me.
Clar. Methoughts that I had broken from the
    Tower
And was embark'd to cross to Burgundy;
And in my company my brother Gloucester,
Who from my cabin tempted me to walk
Upon the hatches. Thence we look'd toward
    England,
And cited up a thousand heavy times,
During the wars of York and Lancaster,
That had befall'n us. As we pac'd along
Upon the giddy footing of the hatches,
Methought that Gloucester stumbled, and in
    falling
Struck me, that thought to stay him,
    overboard
Into the tumbling billows of the main.
O Lord, methought what pain it was to
    drown,

What dreadful noise of waters in my ears,
What sights of ugly death within my eyes!
Methoughts I saw a thousand fearful wrecks,
A thousand men that fishes gnaw'd upon,
Wedges of gold, great anchors, heaps of
        pearl,
Inestimable stones, unvalued jewels,
All scatt'red in the bottom of the sea;
Some lay in dead men's skulls, and in the
        holes
Where eyes did once inhabit there were
        crept,
As 'twere in scorn of eyes, reflecting gems,
That woo'd the slimy bottom of the deep
And mock'd the dead bones that lay scatt'red
        by.

                    Richard III

Portrait of Shakespeare from an early
collection of his works

❧ FORTUNE ❧

Jul.

O Fortune, Fortune! all men call thee
fickle.
If thou art fickle, what dost thou with him
That is renown'd for faith? Be fickle,
Fortune;
For then, I hope, thou wilt not keep him
long,
But send him back.

Romeo and Juliet

Ham.

M y excellent good friends! How dost thou, Guildenstern? Ah, Rosencrantz! Good lads, how do you both?

Ros. As the indifferent children of the earth.

Guil. Happy in that we are not over-happy; On fortune's cap we are not the very button.

      Ham. Nor the soles of her shoe?

Ros. Neither, my lord.

Ham. Then you live about her waist, or in the middle of her favours?

Guil. Faith, her privates we.

Ham. In the secret parts of Fortune? O, most true; she is a strumpet. What news?

Hamlet

Beatrice and Benedick from *Much Ado About Nothing*

Kent.

G ood King, that must approve the
common saw,
Thou out of heaven's benediction com'st
To the warm sun!
Approach, thou beacon to this under globe,
That by thy comfortable beams I may
Peruse this letter. Nothing almost sees miracles
But misery. I know 'tis from Cordelia,
Who hath most fortunately been inform'd
Of my obscured course. [*reads*] '– and shall
find time
From this enormous state – seeking to give
Losses their remedies.' All weary and o'er-
watch'd,
Take vantage, heavy eyes, not to behold
This shameful lodging.
Fortune, good night; smile once more; turn
thy wheel. [*He sleeps.*
King Lear

Edg.

Yet better thus and known to be contemn'd,
Than still contemn'd and flatter'd. To be
worst,
The lowest and most dejected thing of
fortune,
Stands still in esperance, lives not in fear.
The lamentable change is from the best;
The worst returns to laughter. Welcome,
then,
Thou unsubstantial air that I embrace!
The wretch that thou hast blown unto the
worst
Owes nothing to thy blasts.

King Lear

Cleo.

My desolation does begin to make
A better life. 'Tis paltry to be Caesar:
Not being Fortune, he's but Fortune's
          knave,
A minister of her will; and it is great
To do that thing that ends all other deeds,
Which shackles accidents and bolts up
          change,
Which sleeps, and never palates more the
          dug,
The beggar's nurse and Caesar's.

                    Antony and Cleopatra

Dogb.

C ome hither, neighbour Seacoal. God
hath bless'd you with a good name.
To be a well-favoured man is the gift of
fortune; but to write and read comes by
nature.

Much Ado About Nothing

The death of Antony

Bast. Mad world! mad kings! mad composition!
John, to stop Arthur's title in the whole,
Hath willingly departed with a part;
And France, whose armour conscience buckled
             on,
Whom zeal and charity brought to the field
As God's own soldier, rounded in the ear
With that same purpose-changer, that sly devil,
That broker that still breaks the pate of faith,
That daily break-vow, he that wins of all,
Of kings, of beggars, old men, young men, maids,
Who having no external thing to lose
But the word 'maid', cheats the poor maid of that;
That smooth-fac'd gentleman, tickling
             commodity,
Commodity, the bias of the world –
The world, who of itself is peised well,
Made to run even upon even ground,
Till this advantage, this vile-drawing bias,
This sway of motion, this commodity

Makes it take head from all indifferency,
From all direction, purpose, course, intent –
And this same bias, this commodity,
This bawd, this broker, this all-changing word,
Clapp'd on the outward eye of fickle France,
Hath drawn him from his own determin'd aid,
From a resolv'd and honourable war,
To a most base and vile-concluded peace.
And why rail I on this commodity?
But for because he hath not woo'd me yet;
Not that I have the power to clutch my hand
When his fair angels would salute my palm,
But for my hand, as unattempted yet,
Like a poor beggar raileth on the rich.
Well, whiles I am a beggar, I will rail
And say there is no sin but to be rich;
And being rich, my virtue then shall be
To say there is no vice but beggary.
Since kings break faith upon commodity,
Gain, be my lord, for I will worship thee.

King John

Ariel's Song, from *The Tempest*

❧ LIFE ❧

Jaq.   All the world's a stage,
And all the men and women merely players;
They have their exists and their entrances;
And one man in his time plays many parts,
His acts being seven ages. At first the infant,
Mewling and puking in the nurse's arms;
Then the whining school-boy, with his
                satchel
And shining morning face, creeping like snail
Unwillingly to school. And then the lover,
Sighing like furnace, with a woeful ballad
Made to his mistress' eyebrow. Then a
                soldier,

Full of strange oaths, and bearded like the
    pard,
Jealous in honour, sudden and quick in
    quarrel,
Seeking the bubble reputation
Even in the cannon's mouth. And then the
    justice,
In fair round belly with good capon lin'd,
With eyes severe and beard of formal cut,
Full of wise saws and modern instances;
And so he plays his part. The sixth age shifts
Into the lean and slipper'd pantaloon,
With spectacles on nose and pouch on side,

His youthful hose, well sav'd, a world too
        wide
For his shrunk shank; and his big manly
        voice,
Turning again toward childish treble, pipes
And whistles in his sound. Last scene of all,
That ends this strange eventful history,
Is second childishness and mere oblivion;
Sans teeth, sans eyes, sans taste, sans every
        thing.

As You Like It

Lew.

There's nothing in this world can make
me joy.
Life is as tedious as a twice-told tale
Vexing the dull ear of a drowsy man;
And bitter shame hath spoil'd the sweet
world's taste,
That it yields nought but shame and
bitterness.

King John

Public life in Shakespeare's time

T o-morrow, and to-morrow, and to-
    morrow,
Creeps in this petty pace from day to day
To the last syllable of recorded time,
And all our yesterdays have lighted fools
The way to dusty death. Out, out, brief
            candle!
Life's but a walking shadow, a poor player,
That struts and frets his hour upon the stage,
And then is heard no more; it is a tale
Told by an idiot, full of sound and fury,
Signifying nothing.

Macbeth

                    Nothing in his life
Became him like the leaving it: he died
As one that had been studied in his death
To throw away the dearest thing he ow'd
As 'twere a careless trifle.
Dun.   There's no art
To find the mind's construction in the face.
He was a gentleman on whom I built
An absolute trust.

                                        Macbeth

The death of Lear

– My lord, I will take my leave of you.
Ham. You cannot, sir, take from me
anything that I will more willingly
part withal
– except my life, except my life, except my
life.

Hamlet

Ant.

This was the noblest Roman of them all.
  All the conspirators save only he
Did that they did in envy of great Cæsar;
He only in a general honest thought
And common good to all made one of them.
His life was gentle; and the elements
So mix'd in him that Nature might stand up
And say to all the world 'This was a man!'

Julius Caesar

Song.

Gui. Fear no more the heat o' th' sun
     Nor the furious winter's rages;
Thou thy wordly task hast done,
     Home art gone, and ta'en thy wages.
Golden lads and girls all must,
As chimney-sweepers, come to dust.

Arv. Fear no more the frown o' th' great;
     Thou art past the tyrant's stroke.
Care no more to clothe and eat;
     To thee the reed is as the oak.
The sceptre, learning, physic, must
All follow this and come to dust.

Gui.	Fear no more the lightning flash,
Arv.	Nor th' all-dreaded thunder-stone;
Gui.	Fear not slander, censure rash;
Arv.	Thou hast finish'd joy and moan.
Both.	All lovers young, all lovers must
	Consign to thee and come to dust.
Gui.	No exorciser harm thee!
Arv.	Nor no witchcraft charm thee!
Gui.	Ghost unlaid forbear thee!
Arv.	Nothing ill come near thee!
Both.	Quiet consummation have,
	And renowned by thy grave!

Cymbeline

Stratford High Street in the 19th century

Host.

Nay, sure, he's not in hell: he's in Arthur's bosom, if ever man went to Arthur's bosom. 'A made a finer end, and went away an it had been any christom child; 'a parted ev'n just between twelve and one, ev'n at the turning o' th' tide; for after I saw him fumble with the sheets, and play with flowers, and smile upon his fingers' end, I knew there was but one way; for his nose was as sharp as a pen, and 'a babbl'd of green fields. 'How now, Sir John!' quoth I 'What, man, be o' good cheer.' So 'a cried out 'God, God, God!' three or four times. Now I, to comfort him, bid him 'a should not think of God; I hop'd there was no need to trouble himself with any such thoughts yet. So 'a bade me lay more clothes on his feet; I put my hand into the bed and felt them, and they were as cold as any stone; then I felt to his knees, and so upward and upward, and all was as cold as any stone.

Henry V

Shakespeare and his creations

&. AGE .&

Clown sings.

W hen that I was and a little tiny boy,
   With hey, ho, the wind and the rain,
A foolish thing was but a toy,
   For the rain it raineth every day.

But when I came to man's estate,
   With hey, ho, the wind and the rain,
'Gainst knaves and thieves men shut their
         gate,
   For the rain it raineth every day.

But when I came, alas! to wive,
   With hey, ho, the wind and the rain,
By swaggering could I never thrive,
   For the rain it raineth every day.

But when I came unto my beds,
    With hey, ho, the wind and the rain,
With toss-pots still had drunken heads,
    For the rain it raineth every day.

A great while ago the world begun,
    With hey, ho, the wind and the rain,
But that's all one, our play is done,
    And we'll strive to please you every day.
                                    [*Exit.*
                                Twelfth Night

I have liv'd long enough. My way of life
Is fall'n into the sear, the yellow leaf;
And that which should accompany old age,
As honour, love, obedience, troops of
           friends,
I must not look to have; but, in their stead,
Curses not loud but deep, mouth-honour,
           breath,
Which the poor heart would fain deny, and
           dare not.

Macbeth

Dogb.

A good old man, sir, he will be talking; as they say 'When the age is in the wit is out'.

Much Ado About Nothing

Ophelia by the brook, from *Hamlet*

Prince.

Swearest thou, ungracious boy? Hence-
forth ne'er look on me. Thou art
violently carried away from grace; there is
a devil haunts thee in the likeness of an old
fat man; a tun of man is thy companion.
Why dost thou converse with that trunk of
humours, that bolting-hutch of beastliness,
that swoll'n parcel of dropsies, that huge
bombard of sack, that stuff'd cloak-bag of
guts, that roasted Manningtree ox with the
pudding in his belly, that reverend vice, that
grey iniquity, that father ruffian, that vanity
in years? Wherein is he good, but to taste
sack and drink it? wherein neat and cleanly,
but to carve a capon and eat it? wherein
cunning, but in craft? wherein crafty, but in
villainy? wherein villainous, but in all things?
wherein worthy, but in nothing?

Henry IV Part I

Fal.

I would your Grace would take me with
you; whom means your Grace?

Prince. That villainous abominable misleader
of youth, Falstaff, that old white-bearded
Satan.

Fal. My lord, the man I know.

Prince. I know thou dost.

Fal. But to say I know more harm in him
than in myself were to say more than I know.
That he is old – the more the pity – his white
hairs do witness it; but that he is – saving
your reverence – a whoremaster, that I
utterly deny. If sack and sugar be a fault,
God help the wicked! If to be old and merry
be a sin, then many an old host that I know is
damn'd; if to be fat be to be hated, then
Pharaoh's lean kine are to be loved. No, my
good lord: banish Peto, banish Bardolph,
banish Poins; but, for sweet Jack Falstaff,

Monument to Shakespeare in Stratford
Church

kind Jack Falstaff, true Jack Falstaff, valiant Jack Falstaff – and therefore more valiant, being, as he is, old Jack Falstaff – banish not him thy Harry's company, banish not him thy Harry's company. Banish plump Jack, and banish all the world.

Prince. I do, I will.   [*A knocking heard.*
    [*Exeunt Hostess, Francis, and Bardolph.*
    Henry IV Part I

W hen forty winters shall besiege thy
     brow,
And dig deep trenches in thy beauty's field,
Thy youth's proud livery, so gazed on now,
Will be a tatter'd weed, of small worth held:
Then being ask'd where all thy beauty lies,

Where all the treasure of thy lusty days,
To say, within thine own deep-sunken eyes,
Were an all-eating shame and thriftless praise.
How much more praise deserved thy
          beauty's use,
If thou couldst answer 'This fair child of mine
Shall sum my count and make my old excuse,'
Proving his beauty by succession thine!
    This were to be new made when thou art
          old,
    And see thy blood warm when thou feel'st
          it cold.

Ch. Just.

Do you set down your name in the scroll of youth, that are written down old with all the characters of age? Have you not a moist eye, a dry hand, a yellow cheek, a white beard, a decreasing leg, an increasing belly? Is not your voice broken, your wind short, your chin double, your wit single, and every part about you blasted with antiquity? And will you yet call yourself young? Fie, fie, fie, Sir John!

Fal.

M y lord, I was born about three of the clock in the afternoon, with a white head and something a round belly. For my voice – I have lost it with hallooing and singing of anthems. To approve my youth further, I will not. The truth is, I am only old in judgement and understanding; and he that will caper with me for a thousand marks, let him lend me the money, and have at him. For the box of the ear that the Prince gave you – he gave it like a rude prince, and you took it like a sensible lord. I have check'd him for it; and the young lion repents – marry, not in ashes and sack-cloth, but in new silk and old sack.

Henry IV Part II

Gon.   Hear me, my lord:
What need you five and twenty, ten, or five,
To follow in a house where twice so many
Have a command to tend you?
Reg.   What need one?
Lear. O, reason not the need! Our basest
          beggars
Are in the poorest thing superfluous.
Allow not nature more than nature needs,
Man's life is cheap as beast's. Thou art a lady;
If only to go warm were gorgeous,
Why, nature needs not what thou gorgeous
          wear'st,
Which scarcely keeps thee warm. But, for
          true need –
You heavens, give me that patience, patience
          I need.
You see me here, you gods, a poor old man,

As full of grief as age; wretched in both.
If it be you that stirs these daughters' hearts
Against their father, fool me not so much
To bear it tamely; touch me with noble
               anger,
And let not women's weapons, water-drops,
Stain my man's cheeks! No, you unnatural
               hags,
I will have such revenges on you both
That all the world shall – I will do such
               things –
What they are yet I know not; but they shall
               be
The terrors of the earth. You think I'll weep.
No, I'll not weep.   [*Storm and tempest.*
I have full cause of weeping; but this heart
Shall break into a hundred thousand flaws
Or ere I'll weep. O fool, I shall go mad!
     [*Exeunt Lear, Gloucester, Kent, and Fool.*
                              King Lear

T he barge she sat in, like a burnish'd
throne,
Burn'd on the water. The poop was beaten gold;
Purple the sails, and so perfumed that
The winds were love-sick with them; the
oars were silver,
Which to the tune of flutes kept stroke, and
made
The water which they beat to follow faster,
As amorous of their strokes. For her own person,
It beggar'd all description. She did lie
In her pavilion, cloth-of-gold, of tissue,
O'erpicturing that Venus where we see
The fancy out-work nature. On each side her
Stood pretty dimpled boys, like smiling
Cupids,
With divers-colour'd fans, whose wind did seem
To glow the delicate cheeks which they did
cool,
And what they undid did.

    Her gentlewomen, like the Nereides,
So many mermaids, tended her i' th' eyes,
And made their bends adornings. At the helm
A seeming mermaid steers. The silken tackle
Swell with the touches of those flower-soft hands
That yarely frame the office. From the barge
A strange invisible perfume hits the sense
Of the adjacent wharfs. The city cast
Her people out upon her; and Antony,
Enthron'd i' th' market-place, did sit alone,
Whistling to th' air; which, but for vacancy,
Had gone to gaze on Cleopatra too,
And made a gap in nature.

Age cannot wither her, nor custom stale
Her infinite variety. Other women cloy
The appetites they feed, but she makes hungry
Where most she satisfies; for vilest things
Become themselves in her, that the holy priests
Bless her when she is riggish.

Antony and Cleopatra

🍃 TIME 🍃

Ulyss.

Time hath, my lord, a wallet at his back,
    Wherein he puts alms for oblivion,
A great-siz'd monster of ingratitudes.
Those scraps are good deeds past, which are
        devour'd
As fast as they are made, forgot as soon
As done. Perseverance, dear my lord,
Keeps honour bright. To have done is to
        hang
Quite out of fashion, like a rusty mail
In monumental mock'ry. Take the instant
        way;
For honour travels in a strait so narrow

Where one but goes abreast. Keep then the
　　　　　path,
For emulation hath a thousand sons
That one by one pursue; if you give way,
Or hedge aside from the direct forthright,
Like to an ent'red tide they all rush by
And leave you hindmost;
Or, like a gallant horse fall'n in first rank,
Lie there for pavement to the abject rear,
O'er-run and trampled on. Then what they
　　　　　do in present,
Though less than yours in past, must o'ertop
　　　　　yours;
For Time is like a fashionable host,

That slightly shakes his parting guest by th'
            hand;
And with his arms out-stretch'd, as he would
            fly,
Grasps in the comer. The welcome ever smiles,
And farewell goes out sighing. O, let not
            virtue seek
Remuneration for the thing it was;
For beauty, wit,
High birth, vigour of bone, desert in service,
Love, friendship, charity, are subjects all
To envious and calumniating Time.
One touch of nature makes the whole world
            kin —
That all with one consent praise new-born
            gawds,
Though they are made and moulded of things
            past,
And give to dust that is a little gilt
More laud than gilt o'er-dusted.

The present eye praises the present object.
Then marvel not, thou great and complete
      man,
That all the Greeks begin to worship Ajax,
Since things in motion sooner catch the eye
Than what stirs not. The cry went once on
      thee,
And still it might, and yet it may again,
If thou wouldst not entomb thyself alive
And case thy reputation in thy tent,
Whose glorious deeds but in these fields of
      late
Made emulous missions 'mongst the gods
      themselves,
And drave great Mars to faction.

                Troilus and Cressida

Glo.

These late eclipses in the sun and moon portend no good to us. Though the wisdom of nature can reason it thus and thus, yet nature finds itself scourg'd by the sequent effects: love cools, friendship falls off, brothers divide; in cities, mutinies; in countries, discord; in palaces, treason; and the bond crack'd 'twixt son and father. This villain of mine comes under the prediction: there's son against father.

The King falls from bias of nature: there's father against child. We have seen the best of our time: machinations, hollowness, treachery, and all ruinous disorders, follow us disquietly to our graves. Find out this villian, Edmund; it shall lose thee nothing; do it carefully. And the noble and true-hearted Kent banish'd! His offence, honesty! 'Tis strange.   [*Exit.*

King Lear

Prince.

I know you all, and will awhile uphold
The unyok'd humour of your idleness;
Yet herein will I imitate the sun,
Who doth permit the base contagious clouds
To smother up his beauty from the world,
That, when he please again to be himself,
Being wanted, he may be more wond'red at
By breaking through the foul and ugly mists
Of vapours that did seem to strangle him.
If all the year were playing holidays,
To sport would be as tedious as to work;

But when they seldom come, they wish'd-
      for come,
And nothing pleaseth but rare accidents.
So, when this loose behaviour I throw off
And pay the debt I never promised,
By how much better than my word I am,
By so much shall I falsify men's hopes;
And, like bright metal on a sullen ground,
My reformation, glitt'ring o'er my fault,
Shall show more goodly and attract more
      eyes
Than that which hath no foil to set it off.
I'll so offend to make offence a skill,
Redeeming time when men think least I
      will.   [*Exit.*
                Henry IV Part I

W hen I do count the clock that tells
the time,
And see the brave day sunk in hideous night;
When I behold the violet past prime,
And sable curls all silver'd o'er with white;
When lofty trees I see barren of leaves
Which erst from heat did canopy the herd,
And summer's green, all girded up in sheaves,
Borne on the bier with white and bristly
beard;
Then of thy beauty do I question make,
That thou among the wastes of time must go,

Since sweets and beauties do themselves
forsake
And die as fast as they see others grow;
And nothing 'gainst Time's scythe can
make defence
Save breed, to brave him when he takes
thee hence.

Against that time, if ever that time come,
When I shall see thee frown on my defects,
When as they love hath cast his utmost sum,
Call'd to that audit by advised respects;
Against that time when thou shalt strangely
        pass,
And scarcely greet me with that sun, thine
        eye,
When love, converted from the thing it was,
Shall reasons find of settled gravity;
Against that time do I ensconce me here
Within the knowledge of mine own desert,
And this my hand against myself uprear,
To guard the lawful reasons on thy part:
    To leave poor me thou hast the strength
       of laws,
    Since why to love I can allege no cause.

Like as the waves make towards the pebbled
               shore,
So do our minutes hasten to their end;
Each changing place with that which goes
               before,
In sequent toil all forwards do contend.
Nativity, once in the main of light,
Crawls to maturity, wherewith being
               crown'd,
Crooked eclipses 'gainst his glory fight,
And Time that gave doth now his gift
               confound.
Time doth transfix the flourish set on youth
And delves the parallels in beauty's brow,
Feeds on the rarities of nature's truth,
And nothing stands but for his scythe to
               mow:
   And yet to times in hope my verse shall
               stand,
   Praising thy worth, despite his cruel hand.

When I have seen by Time's fell hand
            defaced
The rich proud cost of outworn buried age;
When sometime lofty towers I see down-
            razed
And brass eternal slave to mortal rage;
When I have seen the hungry ocean gain
Advantage on the kingdom of the shore,
And the firm soil win of the watery main,
Increasing store with loss and loss with store;
When I have seen such interchange of state,
Or state itself confounded to decay;
Ruin hath taught me thus to ruminate,
That Time will come and take my love
            away.
    This thought is as a death, which cannot
            choose
    But weep to have that which it fears to
            lose.

Music do I hear?
Ha, ha! keep time. How sour sweet music is
When time is broke and no proportion kept!
So is it in the music of men's lives.
And here have I the daintiness of ear
To check time broke in a disorder'd string;
But, for the concord of my state and time,
Had not an ear to hear my true time broke.
I wasted time, and now doth time waste me;
For now hath time made me his numb'ring
          clock:
My thoughts are minutes; and with sighs
          they jar
Their watches on unto mine eyes, the
          outward watch,
Whereto my finger, like a dial's point,
Is pointing still, in cleansing them from tears.

Now, sir, the sound that tells what hour it is
Are clamorous groans which strike upon my
heart,
Which is the bell. So sighs, and tears, and
groans,
Show minutes, times, and hours; but my
time
Runs posting on in Bolingbroke's proud joy,
While I stand fooling here, his Jack of the
clock.
This music mads me. Let it sound no more;
For though it have holp madmen to their
wits,
In me it seems it will make wise men mad.
                                        Richard II